Parkman Congregational
Church Library
18265 Madison Rd., Box 655
Parkman, OH 44080

Room in the Stable

written by
Crystal BOWMAN

illustrated by
Beverly LUEDECKE

music by
Lynn HODGES

Equipping Kids for Life!
faithkids.com

Faith Parenting Guide
Ages 10 months & up
Bible Knowledge

A Faith Parenting Guide
can be found on page 32.

Faith Kids® is an imprint of Cook Communications Ministries
Colorado Springs, Colorado 80918
Cook Communications, Paris, Ontario
Kingsway Communications, Eastbourne, England

Room in the Stable
©2002 by Crystal Bowman for text, Lynn Hodges for music, and Beverly Luedecke for illustrations

First printing, 2002
Printed in Singapore.
1 2 3 4 5 6 7 8 9 10 Printing/Year 06 05 04 03 02

Editor: Heather Gemmen
Designer: Dana Sherrer, iDesignEtc.

Library of Congress Cataloging-in-Publication Data

Bowman, Crystal.
   Room in the stable / written by Crystal Bowman ; music by Lynn Hodges ; illustrated by Beverly Luedecke.
      p. cm.
   Summary: Rhyming story about the animals who welcomed Jesus in the stable in Bethlehem.
   ISBN 0-7814-3797-0
   1. Jesus Christ--Nativity--Juvenile fiction. [1. Jesus
Christ--Nativity--Fiction. 2. Stories in rhyme.]   I. Hodges, Lynn. II. Luedecke, Bev, ill. III. Title.
   PZ8.3.B6773 Ro 2002
   [E]--dc21   2001004403

One chilly night as the
sun floated down,
The stable animals
gathered around.

4

The cow began munching
on golden hay;
The birds found their perch
while the cat purred away.

6

But something exciting stirred in the air.

The cows and the sheep could sense it was there.

What was it? they wondered. *What could it be?*

They patiently waited and hoped they would see.

Then Donkey announced,
   "There are travelers in town;
Children and grown-ups
   are walking around

8

Searching for food and places
to sleep.
Perhaps they'll stay here with
the cows and the sheep."

The animals said,

"We'd be happy to share

Our stable and hay with the

people out there."

11

"We've plenty of room where
travelers can rest.
We'll share all we have
and give them our best."

The cows began singing
their evening song.
Baa, went the lamb
as he right sang along.

14

15

Then up from the path a couple came near.

The man told his wife, "We'll have to stop here.

There's room in the stable. It's where we must stay.

We need to lie down and rest in the hay."

17

And just when the travelers were cozy and warm,

A miracle happened. A baby was born!

They wrapped him in blankets and cradled his head,

Then put him to sleep in a soft manger bed.

19

The creatures were quiet,
the night air was still,
While shepherds were resting
nearby on a hill.

20

21

Then all of a sudden
some angels appeared.
The shepherds were startled
and trembled with fear.
"Don't be afraid,"
said the angels to them.

"Our Savior's been born in
Bethlehem."
An army of angels filled
the whole sky
Singing, "Glory to God,
Almighty, Most High!"

24

The angels soon vanished into the night,
   While the stars in the sky twinkled so bright.
The shepherds hurried and ran all the way,
   Until they found Jesus asleep on the hay.

25

After they saw him,
they told everyone
The wonderful news of
God's only Son.

They went out rejoicing,
"Give thanks and sing,
For we have worshiped
the newborn King!"

It's fun to pretend what
the animals said
As the little Lord Jesus
slept in his bed.
The Bible tells
of our Savior's birth—

How Jesus, God's Son,

was sent down to Earth.

He came to bring peace,

salvation, and love.

And now he's with God

in heaven above.

Room in the Stable

Words by Beverly Leudecke
Music by Lynn Hodges

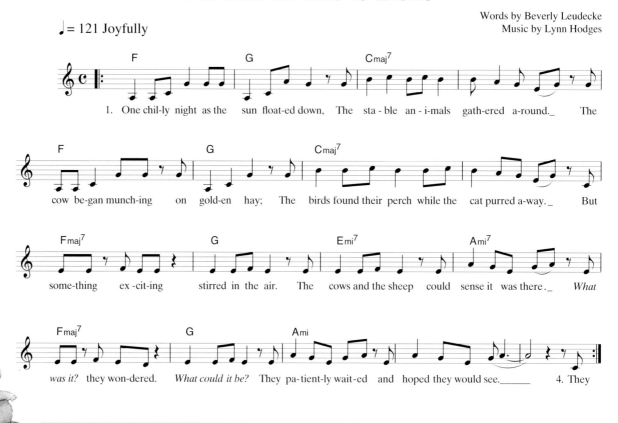

♩ = 121 Joyfully

1. One chil-ly night as the sun float-ed down, The sta - ble an - i-mals gath-ered a-round._ The

cow be-gan munch-ing on gold-en hay; The birds found their perch while the cat purred a-way._ But

some-thing ex -cit-ing stirred in the air. The cows and the sheep could sense it was there._ *What*

was it? they won-dered. What could it be? They pa-tient-ly wait-ed and hoped they would see._____ 4. They

30

Slower

wrapped him in blank-ets   and   cra-dled his head, then   put him to sleep in a   soft man-ger bed._____ The

crea-tures were qui-et,   the   night air was still, While shep-herds were rest-ing near- by on a hill._   Then

all   of a -sud-den   some an - gels ap-peared.   The   shep-herds were star-tled   and   trem-bled with fear._

2. Then Donkey announced, "There are travelers in town; Children and grown-ups are walking around Searching for food and places to sleep. Perhaps they'll stay here with the cows and the sheep." The animals said, "We'd be happy to share Our stable and hay with the people out there. We've plenty of room where travelers can rest. We'll share all we have and give them our best."

3. The cows began singing their evening song. *Baa*, went the lamb as he sang right along. Then up from the path a couple came near. The mad told his wife, "We'll have to stop here. There's room in the stable. It's where we must stay. We need to lie down and rest in the hay." And just when the travelers were cozy and warm, a miracle happened. A baby was born!

Room in the Stable

Life Issue: I want my children to love the Christmas story.

Spiritual Building Block: Bible knowledge

Help your children to enjoy the true meaning of Christmas in the following ways:

Sight: Go all out with decorations in and around your home. Drive to streets that are known for their dazzling Christmas lights. Wrap the Christmas presents beautifully. Tell your children that one of the very best, most important, and happiest holidays is just around the corner: Jesus' birthday party. Enthusiastically explain that your family will honor God's gift of his Son to us by celebrating it with gusto.

Sound: As Christmas approaches, enjoy with your children the many wonderful Christmas storybooks. Read them after dinner, at bedtime, on a snowy Saturday afternoon, and before church on a Sunday morning. Let your children tell you their own versions of the Christmas story, and listen attentively. Tell them the story as you are driving, making pancakes, or waiting in line. Then, on Christmas morning, read with great expression and excitement the very best version of all: the biblical account.

Touch: As you and your children decorate the Christmas tree this year, talk about the symbolism of each ornament. Videotape your children as they take turns holding up different ornaments to talk about how each one reminds them of the Christmas story. And then let your children hang the ornaments on the tree all by themselves.